WISDOM

THOUGHTS AND QUOTATIONS FOR EVERY DAY

summersdale

Summersdale Publishers Ltd
46 West Street
Chichester
West Sussex
PO19 1RP
UK

www.summersdale.com

Printed and bound in the Czech Republic

ISBN: 978-1-78685-241-0

Substantial discounts on bulk quantities of Summersdale books are available to corporations, professional associations and other organisations. For details contact general enquiries: telephone: +44 (0) 1243 771107 or email: enquiries@summersdale.com.

To ....

From ....

Make each day
both useful and
pleasant, and prove
that you understand
the worth of time by
employing it well.

Louisa May Alcott

Knowledge
comes but
wisdom lingers.

Alfred, Lord Tennyson

It takes courage to face one's own shortcomings, and wisdom to do something about them.

Edgar Cayce

Our lives begin to end the day we become silent about things that matter.

Martin Luther King Jr

LIFE IS LIKE RIDING A BICYCLE. TO KEEP YOUR BALANCE YOU MUST KEEP MOVING.

Albert Einstein

Courage is what it takes to stand up and speak. Courage is also what it takes to sit down and listen.

Winston Churchill

THERE ARE THREE INGREDIENTS IN THE GOOD LIFE: LEARNING, EARNING AND YEARNING.

Christopher Morley

We carry within us the wonders we seek without us.

Thomas Browne

THE ONLY GIFT
IS A PORTION
OF THYSELF.

Ralph Waldo Emerson

YOU MUST BE
THE CHANGE
YOU WISH
TO SEE IN
THE WORLD.

Mahatma Gandhi

The greater
the obstacle, the
more glory in
overcoming it.

Molière

The more we see,
the more we are
capable of seeing.

Maria Mitchell

WE ARE MADE WISE NOT
BY THE RECOLLECTION
OF OUR PAST, BUT BY
THE RESPONSIBILITY
FOR OUR FUTURE.

George Bernard Shaw

WISE MEN
LEARN MANY
THINGS FROM
THEIR ENEMIES.

Aristophanes

True religion is real
living; living with
all one's soul, with
all one's goodness
and righteousness.

Albert Einstein

THE MOST DECISIVE
ACTIONS OF OUR
LIFE... ARE, MORE
OFTEN THAN NOT,
UNCONSIDERED.

André Gide

Be happy.
It's one way of
being wise.

Colette

THE WISE MAN DOES AT ONCE WHAT THE FOOL DOES FINALLY.

Niccolo Machiavelli

IF YOUR COMPASSION DOES NOT INCLUDE YOURSELF, IT IS INCOMPLETE.

Jack Kornfield

The art of
BEING WISE
is knowing what to
OVERLOOK.

William James

To be what we are,
and to become what
we are capable of
becoming, is the
only end of life.

Robert Louis Stevenson

WE LEARN
WISDOM FROM
FAILURE MUCH
MORE THAN
SUCCESS.

Samuel Smiles

It is not because
things are difficult
that we do not dare;
it is because we do
not dare that they
are difficult.

Seneca

BY ATTEMPTING
THE
IMPOSSIBLE
ONE CAN
ATTAIN THE
HIGHEST
LEVEL OF THE
POSSIBLE.

August Strindberg

Turn your ear to WISDOM
and apply your
heart to
UNDERSTANDING.

Proverbs 2:2

The highest
result of education
is tolerance.

Helen Keller

The good life is
one inspired by
love and guided
by knowledge.

Bertrand Russell

The longer you can look back, the farther you can look forward.

Winston Churchill

Kindness is more
important than
wisdom, and the
recognition of this
is the beginning
of wisdom.

Theodore Rubin

Only a life lived
for others is a
life worthwhile.

Albert Einstein

IT IS STRANGE
HOW OFTEN
A HEART MUST
BE BROKEN
BEFORE THE
YEARS CAN
MAKE IT WISE.

Sara Teasdale

*Better than
a hundred years of*

IDLENESS

is one day spent in

DETERMINATION.

The Dhammapada

KNOWLEDGE
IS A PROCESS
OF PILING UP
FACTS; WISDOM
LIES IN THEIR
SIMPLIFICATION.

Martin Fischer

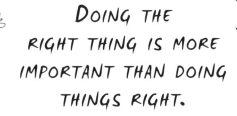

DOING THE
RIGHT THING IS MORE
IMPORTANT THAN DOING
THINGS RIGHT.

Peter Drucker

He who has begun is half done; Dare to be wise; begin.

Horace

Beauty endures only for as long as it can be seen; goodness, beautiful today, will remain so tomorrow.

Sappho

Wonder is
the beginning
of wisdom.

Socrates

A MAN'S
TRUE
WEALTH... IS
THE GOOD
THAT HE
DOES IN THIS
WORLD TO
HIS FELLOWS.

Muhammad

GREAT WORKS ARE PERFORMED NOT BY STRENGTH BUT BY PERSEVERANCE.

Samuel Johnson

Speak few words, but say them with quietude and sincerity and they will be long-lasting.

Lao Tzu

Vanity is the quicksand of reason.

George Sand

Life is so
constructed that
an event does
not, cannot, will
not, match the
expectation.

Charlotte Brontë

ALL HUMAN
WISDOM IS
SUMMED
UP IN TWO
WORDS –
WAIT AND
HOPE.

Alexandre Dumas

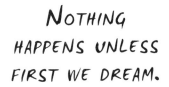

NOTHING HAPPENS UNLESS FIRST WE DREAM.

Carl Sandburg

Life is like playing
a violin solo in
public, and learning
the instrument as one
goes on.

Samuel Butler

Patience is
the companion
of wisdom.

St Augustine
of Hippo

If you do not
tell the truth
about yourself you
cannot tell it about
other people.

Virginia Woolf

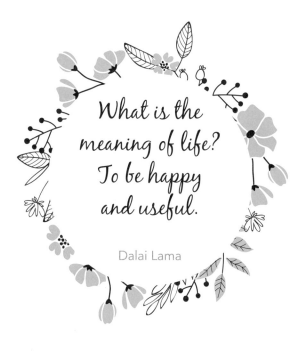

What is the
meaning of life?
To be happy
and useful.

Dalai Lama

IT IS
COWARDICE
TO PERCEIVE
WHAT IS
RIGHT BUT
NOT TO
DO IT.

Confucius

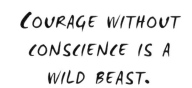

COURAGE WITHOUT
CONSCIENCE IS A
WILD BEAST.

Robert G. Ingersoll

LET YOUR HOOK ALWAYS
BE CAST; IN THE POOL
WHERE YOU LEAST EXPECT
IT, THERE WILL BE FISH.

Ovid

HONOUR HAS NOT TO BE WON: IT MUST ONLY NOT BE LOST.

Arthur Schopenhauer

People grow through
experience if they
meet life honestly
and courageously.
This is how character
is built.

Eleanor Roosevelt

NO ACT OF KINDNESS, NO MATTER HOW SMALL, IS EVER WASTED.

Aesop

REJECT YOUR SENSE OF INJURY AND THE INJURY ITSELF DISAPPEARS.

Marcus Aurelius

ONE MUST
BE POOR
TO KNOW
THE LUXURY
OF GIVING.

George Eliot

When you are
good to others you are
best to yourself.

Benjamin Franklin

He who masters others has STRENGTH. *He who masters himself has* TRUE POWER.

Lao Tzu

Life begets life.
Energy creates
energy. It is by
spending oneself that
one becomes rich.

Sarah Bernhardt

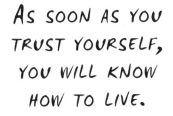

As soon as you trust yourself, you will know how to live.

Johann Wolfgang von Goethe

YOU CANNOT
RUN AWAY
FROM
WEAKNESS;
YOU MUST
SOME TIME
FIGHT IT OUT
OR PERISH.

Robert Louis Stevenson

Don't stumble
over something
behind you.

Seneca the
Younger

If you have
KNOWLEDGE,
let others
LIGHT THEIR
CANDLES
in it.

Margaret Fuller

POWER WITHOUT
WISDOM COLLAPSES
UNDER ITS OWN
WEIGHT.

Horace

The greatest
mistake you can make
in life is to be
continually fearing
you will make one.

Elbert Hubbard

NEVER APOLOGISE FOR SHOWING FEELING. WHEN YOU DO SO, YOU APOLOGISE FOR THE TRUTH.

Benjamin Disraeli

The truest greatness lies in being kind, the truest wisdom in a happy mind.

Ella Wheeler Wilcox

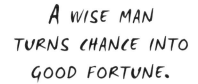

A WISE MAN
TURNS CHANCE INTO
GOOD FORTUNE.

Thomas Fuller

PLEASURE
in the task puts
PERFECTION
in the work.

Aristotle

Memory is
the mother of
all wisdom.

Aeschylus

THE ONLY CERTAINTY IS THAT NOTHING IS CERTAIN.

Pliny the Elder

HE WHO
KNOWS
OTHERS IS
LEARNED; HE
WHO KNOWS
HIMSELF
IS WISE.

Lao Tzu

Life was meant to be lived and curiosity must be kept alive. One must never, for whatever reason, turn his back on life.

Eleanor Roosevelt

WISDOM IS
OFTENTIMES
NEARER WHEN
WE STOOP THAN
WHEN WE SOAR.

William Wordsworth

Anything will give up its SECRETS if you LOVE IT enough.

George Washington Carver

The only true voyage
of discovery would
be not to visit new
lands but to possess
other eyes.

Marcel Proust

FORGIVENESS IS A VIRTUE OF THE BRAVE.

Indira Gandhi

The surest
test of discipline
is its absence.

Clara Barton

HONESTY IS THE FIRST CHAPTER IN THE BOOK OF WISDOM.

Thomas Jefferson

There is not a heart
but has its moments
of longing, yearning
for something better,
nobler, holier than
it knows now.

Henry Ward Beecher

All men by nature
desire knowledge.

Aristotle

To conquer
FEAR
is the beginning of
WISDOM.

Bertrand Russell

To enjoy freedom...
we have to control
ourselves.

Virginia Woolf

A WISE
MAN MAKES
HIS OWN
DECISIONS,
AN IGNORANT
MAN FOLLOWS
THE PUBLIC
OPINION.

Chinese proverb

THINGS DO NOT
HAPPEN. THINGS ARE
MADE TO HAPPEN.

John F. Kennedy

The strongest
principle of growth
lies in human choice.

George Eliot

Without courage,
wisdom bears
no fruit.

Baltasar Gracián

BE FAITHFUL TO THAT WHICH EXISTS NOWHERE BUT IN YOURSELF.

André Gide

There is nothing
IMPOSSIBLE
to him who will
TRY.

Alexander the Great

Listen or your tongue will keep you deaf.

Native American
proverb

BE NOT
AFRAID OF
LIFE. BELIEVE
THAT LIFE IS
WORTH LIVING,
AND YOUR
BELIEF WILL
HELP CREATE
THE FACT.

William James

DO WHAT YOU CAN,
WITH WHAT YOU HAVE,
WHERE YOU ARE.

Theodore Roosevelt

If you're interested in
finding out more about our
books, find us on Facebook
at Summersdale Publishers
and follow us on Twitter
at @Summersdale.

www.summersdale.com